Fragrant Flowers and Foliage

Jasminum polyanthum

Fragrant Flowers and Foliage

Denise Greig

Kangaroo Press

For Penny Greig, with love

Cover: Red Frangipani *(Plumeria rubra)*

First published in 1990 by Kangaroo Press Pty Ltd
3 Whitehall Road (P.O. Box 75) Kenthurst NSW 2156
Typeset by G. T. Setters Pty Limited
Printed in Singapore by Kyodo Printing Co (S'pore) Pte Ltd

ISBN 0 86417 283 4

Contents

Introduction

Fragrance brings joy, sensuality and precious charm to any garden. As well as being pleasing to the eye a garden should delight our sense of smell. There are varying degrees of fragrance from sweet, fruity, floral or heady to the subtle spicy aroma released by some plants when the leaves are crushed or splashed by a shower of rain. Some plants release their scent when the sun is low while others send their scents far out carried on a breeze.

Fragrant plants suit all garden design and there should be space for fragrance even in the smallest garden. You may wish to create your own special scented scheme such as an evening garden, an old fashioned garden, a herb garden or, as many beautifully perfumed plants are white, a white garden. A section of the garden could be devoted to cut flowers or for providing potpourri ingredients. Remember that you produce more prolific flowering if you pick blooms consistently. Sweet peas picked as they flower will reward you with more blooms later in the season. You can even have the fragrance of the Australian bush in your garden with boronias, wattle, mint bush and eucalypts.

This book offers a great selection of perfumed plants including annuals, perennials, bulbs, climbers, shrubs and trees. There are chapters on roses, fragrant herbs, scented geraniums and potpourri. Many native plants with aromatic foliage are also included. You will find most, if not all, of the plants mentioned in any of the major garden centres.

Fragrant plants have been used for thousands of years for reasons both aesthetic and therapeutic. Enjoy the histories and legends of some of these plants while planning and planting your fragrant garden.

Annuals, Biennials and Perennials

An **annual** completes its life cycle in the space of twelve months. Annual flowers with a perfume are not many, but who would be without the sweetness of wallflowers, stocks, and sweet peas to add fragrance to the garden. These flowers have the additional charm of providing a regular supply of cut flowers for the house. Annuals grow rapidly and provide quick colour and fragrance while longer lasting plants are maturing. Some will self sow, such as alyssum and forget-me-nots, and will pop up in future years in unexpected places. Annuals can be used to fill flower beds, massed in drifts, as flower pot plants, trailers in hanging baskets or in window boxes.

It is best to sow annuals in the garden where you want them to flower. Once they reach the seedling stage, thin out the weaker plants to give space and air to the sturdiest. Because the great majority of annual seeds are small in size, it is necessary to clean the soil of weeds and rake the surface to as fine a condition as possible before sowing them directly into position. Carefully rake fine soil over the seeds so that they are just buried and gently water with a fine sprinkler. In a mild climate the seeds of fairly quick growing annuals can be sown outdoors in the autumn, spring and summer. Where severe winters prevail avoid autumn sowing. Alternatively raise seedlings in boxes and transplant to the open ground when all fear of frost is over.

A **biennial** germinates and produces leaves, roots and stems for the first year, then in the second year it still grows, but also produces flowers and seeds, then dies. As they are leafy and without blooms for the first year and many are fairly tall growing they are best treated as background plants in the border.

A **perennial** is a plant with soft stems that lives for three or more years, usually flowering and fruiting each year. Every year the stems die down and the roots remain alive, sending up fresh growth again the following year, usually in spring. The classic herbaceous border so beloved by the English is composed of only perennial plants.

Perennials respond well to feeding. Before planting out fork well into the soil manure or a rich, well rotted compost. Applications of soluble fertilisers during the growing season may also be desirable. Perennials benefit from a surface mulch of fibrous compost, which will also retard weeds and improve the soil.

Not all perennials are fragrant and a strict herbaceous border can require considerable space and maintenance. Perennials mixed with small shrubs, bulbs and annuals with perhaps a background of climbing roses can create an interesting and fragrant garden which is presentable throughout the year and gives the gardener much less work.

Antirrhinum majus **Snapdragon** This perennial is usually grown in numerous cultivated varieties as an annual. There are three height forms: the tall giant-flowered type to 1 m tall which is used as cut flowers; the medium-size variety to 60 cm tall and the dwarf type to around 25 cm high suitable for edgings. The cloying or spicy fragrance of the snapdragon does not appeal to all tastes (or noses), but the wonderful range of colours makes it a desirable garden plant and cut flower. Flowers are produced from early spring to midsummer. Grow in a well drained, medium quality soil in a sunny position.

Calomeria amaranthoides **Incense Plant** This is an Australian biennial known to many people who have country houses in southeastern Australia. It forms a large leafy plant in the first year and produces marvellous plumes of red or reddish-brown flowers up to 3 m tall in the second year. The flowers have a strong incense-like perfume. This interesting species is best used as a background plant in a sunny or partially shaded position. Obtain seedlings or fresh seeds from country friends and provide plenty of water during hot weather.

Cheiranthus cheiri **Common Wallflower** Although a short lived perennial, this is usually grown as an annual or biennial. It is a bushy plant to 75 cm high with yellow-brown warmly perfumed flowers during late winter and spring. Several cultivars in shades of burgundy, brown, crimson, yellow, orange and white are available. Sometimes double flowers are multi-coloured. Fine displays may be obtained by planting in masses or clumps in an open sunny position. Provide plenty of moisture during dry weather.

Dianthus

This genus of some 300 species of annuals, perennials and sub-shrubs includes some of the most fragrant flowers in the world. Cottage pinks and florist's carnations are two great cultivar groups of an ancient garden lineage. *Dianthus caryophyllus*, a parent of the modern carnation, was introduced by the monks of Normandy immediately following the invasion of England in 1066, and it can still be found growing around the ruined walls of many Norman castles and monasteries. It is believed that the old fashioned cottage pinks are largely derived from *D. plumarius*. All species of *Dianthus* require full sun and very good drainage. All do well in sandy loam with the addition of humus or compost.

D. barbatus Sweet William A bushy little plant that is nearly always grown as a biennial and used as a border or edging plant. It develops into a loosely formed mat to no more than 60 cm tall. The small fragrant flowers are borne in broad flattened heads to 8 cm or more across. Their colours range through pink, red, violet and white and some have frilly edges. They bloom during spring and summer and can be used as cut flowers.

D. caryophyllus Carnation The carnation is a hardy perennial plant which provides the fragrant clove scented flowers that are so pleasing as a cut flower. Carnations grow to around 1 m tall with slender, bluish-green leaves and flower stems. The flowers are borne singly and are often double in shades of white, pink, red, purple, yellow, apricot and white. When young plants have been set out and are growing strongly, they should be pinched back at least twice. If large blooms are desired, all the lateral flower buds should be removed to encourage long stems. These stems will probably need staking. When cutting flowers for the house, cut low down on the stem just above a leaf joint. This encourages low new shoots and prevents the plant from becoming too tall.

Take new cuttings each year to ensure a continual supply of plants. The best cuttings are stems taken immediately after flowering. Take pieces about 10 cm long and remove lower leaves. Plant about 3 cm of the lower stem very firmly in damp clean sand. Keep just damp and protect from wind and direct sun. The average time of rooting for cuttings is about six weeks. The best time for planting out rooted cuttings is in late winter and spring and again in autumn.

***D. plumarius* Cottage Pinks** A small perennial to 40 cm tall with narrow leaves and often fringed flowers in rose, purple, white or multi-colours. Cottage pinks make delightful border or edging plants. Place them in the garden about 15 to 20 cm apart. If conditions are right they will last for a few years, however it is a good idea to lift them every couple of years or so and divide them to give them room to breathe. Cottage pinks have a soft spicy scent and their modest size makes them ideal for posies.

***Iberis amara* Candytuft** The annual candytufts are hardy, easily grown and useful for bordering, massed bedding and rockeries. They produce attractive cut flowers which last well indoors. Picking helps prolong the flowering period which is during spring and summer. They grow to a height of around 40 cm and produce sweetly scented white hyacinth-like flowers. Plants do best in light, well drained soils in a sunny position and require a fair amount of moisture during dry weather. Sow seed where they are required to grow and flower either in the autumn or spring. The pink, lilac and crimson types of candytufts are hybrids of *I. umbellata*, the globe or common candytuft, which is the type most widely grown, but does not have the sweet fragrance of *I. amara*.

***Lathyrus odoratus* Sweet Pea** One of the most delightful flowering annuals, the sweet pea was first introduced into cultivation during the 18th century. Breeding since then has produced an enormous range of colours and heights, including dwarf bedding varieties and early flowering forms that are ideal for warmer climates. All are fragrant although some of the more spectacular modern hybrids are less fragrant. Sweet peas need rich deep soil with good drainage but plenty of moisture. Sow seeds where the plants are to bloom in autumn and in cool districts during spring. For climbing varieties provide supports such as trellises, a wire frame or other suitable material prior to planting. A bowl of sweet peas is hard to beat for freshness and fragrance. Pick all blooms when they are opened but before they begin to form seed pods to prolong flower display.

Lobularia maritima **Sweet Alyssum, Sweet Alice** This perennial with a semi-creeping habit is usually grown as an annual. It is popular for its long flowering season and delightfully honey scented flowers. The white variety, which is the tallest to around 20 cm in height, will seed itself profusely in any garden soil, while the named cultivars in shades of purple and pink are lower growing, less scented and tend to revert to white when self-sown. Sow seed directly into the garden and thin out later to about 20 cm apart. The seed is small and should only be lightly covered with fine soil. Should the flowering branches become straggly they may be cut back to encourage the development of another crop.

Matthiola bicornis **Night-scented Stock** This is a fast growing and rather straggly, grey-leaved species with single, rather insignificant flowers in colour tones of pink to purple which open at night in late winter and spring. The flowers are so sweetly scented in the evening that it is worth growing them, especially beneath a window or near a door leading to the garden, for the scent alone. Grow in a well drained soil in a cool, even semi-shaded situation.

Matthiola incana **Stock** These short lived perennials are generally grown as annuals. With very fragrant and beautifully coloured blooms, stocks are grown for garden display and for cut flowers. They are available in many different types and varieties. Some are freely branching; others, called column stocks, develop single unbranched column-like flower stems. Dwarf types grow to about 30 cm high and giants to around 75 cm. All are perfumed. Stocks should never be grown in a soil that has grown stocks the previous year. They need a good organic soil enriched with well decayed manure and compost and a sunny location. The soil must be well drained as stocks will not tolerate wet feet.

Myosotis **Forget-me-not** These are biennials or short lived perennials and are often treated as an annual. They grow to a height of around 40 cm and have delightful small sky-blue flowers which are lightly fragrant. There are cultivars with flowers in shades of pink and white, but it is the lovely blue forget-me-nots that form pretty carpets if left undisturbed in a damp semi-shady part of the garden. They will self-seed freely year by year and excessive seedlings might need to be removed from time to time to keep them within bounds.

Primula malacoides **Fairy Primrose** One of our best winter or early spring flowers for beds, borders, pots, window boxes and table decoration. It is a perennial that is usually grown as an annual. Its pale green leaves grow in rosettes and numerous delicately fragrant flowers are borne in pretty whorls well above the leaves. Flowers are offered in shades of white, pink, crimson and lavender. Plants should be spaced 25 cm apart in the garden and do best in a moist semi-shaded position. They make a striking display when massed and also combine well with spring bulbs.

Primula × *polyantha* **Polyanthus Primrose** These lovely perennials are a horticultural hybrid derived from the common primrose, *P. vulgaris*, the cowslip, *P. veris*, and the oxslip, *P. elatior*. Flowers are sweetly scented and come in a wide range of colours including white, pink, red, yellow and various shades of blue and violet, appearing in winter, spring and summer. They make wonderful edging plants and are stunning in groups in containers. Grow in a rich moist soil in a sheltered partially shaded position. Ensure that those grown in containers do not dry out in hot, dry or windy weather.

Reseda odorata **Mignonette, Little Darling** A charming old fashioned annual that is grown for its exquisite sweet scent. It is a branching plant to no more than 40 cm tall with loose spikes of heavily scented yellowish-white flowers with prominent stamens. Flowers appear in late autumn and through to midsummer. It is advisable to sow the seeds where the plants are to flower as they resent transplanting. The best time for sowing is in late summer, but spring only in cold districts. Seedlings will need thinning to about 30 cm apart. There are a few colourful cultivars offered for sale, but it is the white flowering forms that are more fragrant and attractive.

Viola odorata **Sweet Violet** This well loved garden plant is a spreading perennial which flowers in winter and early spring. With its beautiful fragrance combined with a modest appearance the violet is seen as a symbol of humility and fidelity. It is ideal for bedding, rockeries and outdoor containers and perfect for picking for small posies. For best results violets should be given reasonably good soil and an open situation with some shade in summer. Too much loving care, fertiliser and shade may cause violets to produce leaf growth at the expense of flowers.

The Australian native violet, *Viola hederacea*, a charming but bossy spreading plant, does not have fragrant flowers.

Bulbs and Lilies

The fragrant essence of spring is embodied in the perfect shapes of the flowering bulbs which bring colour and charm to any garden. And for late spring and summer scents no self-respecting fragrant garden would be without the enchantment of at least a few lilies, such as the November lily and the Madonna lily with their lovely waxy white trumpet shaped flowers which smell beautiful and look good even after dark.

According to historians lilies were used as decorations on Cretan pottery and wall paintings more than a thousand years before the Christian era. The Egyptians used lilies in their funeral garlands and bulbs were found in mummy cases. Hyacinths, narcissus and lilies had an important place in the gardens of the early Romans, who valued these flowers for their use in religious ceremonies. The Madonna lily was so highly cherished that it became a symbol of purity in the church and was frequently painted by medieval artists, mostly in connection with religious subjects.

The term bulb has been used generally in this chapter to include both bulbs and corms as well as certain tuberous and rhizomatous plants, any plant in fact that has a swollen rootstock.

If space permits nothing is more delightful than a naturalised patch or drift of spring bulbs just popping up as they wish. Bluebells, freesias, jonquils and grape hyacinths are all adaptable and useful for naturalising and can be left undisturbed to multiply for years to their heart's content. Most like cool conditions and their roots sheltered, so they do well under trees or between shrubs in semi-shade. After three to five years or when flowers become fewer or small it is time to lift and divide the clumps. Do this as soon as the leaves have died down.

For the smaller garden or in a mixed border, bulbs always look their best when planted in clumps. To achieve dramatic effects and to enjoy the brilliant colours consider a part of the garden with an attractive lush foliage background. Smaller bulbs such as snowdrops and hyacinths need to be planted well to the foreground, while a cluster of lilies makes a striking accent planted further back. For colour, fragrance and exquisite sprays of cut flowers do not overlook the highly perfumed multi-coloured freesias, which will give any garden an unforgetable early spring fragrance.

Bulbs look brilliant in containers for balconies, verandahs, roof gardens, window gardens, courtyards and indoors, if there is sufficient light. Pots, bowls, troughs and containers of all types are suitable for growing bulbs and will provide instant colour, fragrance and life for every nook and cranny. Many of the best spring flowering bulbs can be grown to perfection in containers in a commercial preparation of fibre.

The main planting time for spring flowering bulbs is late summer and early autumn, but the season can be extended to late autumn if circumstances delay earlier planting. Bulbs like a well drained soil. A well nourished soil is necessary, but bulbs object to coming in contact with any fresh manure at planting time. If possible, prepare a bed of well rotted manure, well rotted compost or other organic material at least five weeks before planting. If the soil is not in the best condition at planting time provide a good surface mulch of mixed compost. Later water occasionally with liquid fertiliser or manure. Ensure that bulbs are planted the right way up. The depth for planting individual species varies, but a good general rule is to plant at a depth of twice to three times the bulb's own depth.

When cutting flowers, leave as much foliage as possible for the leaves provide nutrient to be stored in the bulb to nourish next season's growth and flower production. Never cut back the leaves when flowering has finished, but wait until the foliage has turned yellow and withered. If this looks too unattractive for a small garden provide an overplanting of sweet Alice or forget-me-nots.

Convallaria majalis **Lily of the Valley** The dainty, sweetly fragrant lily of the valley has been a treasured garden plant since Elizabethan times and has been used as a popular cut flower, in perfume, medicine and as an excellent dye plant. It forms a thick carpet of broad green leaves and in early spring sends up delicate stalks of fragrant white bell shaped flowers. This native of Europe grows best in districts with a cool to cold winter, in a shaded or partially shaded position. It thrives in a good soil enriched with decayed manure, leaf mould or compost. Plants can be left undisturbed for many years but should be divided when the roots become overcrowded.

Crinum

The name *Crinum* is derived from the Greek *krunum*, meaning lily, although strictly they do not belong to the lily family. They are stately plants and produce showy lily-like flowers, mostly in late spring and summer, which are usually fragrant and come in shades of pink and white. They do well in temperate regions and require a well drained, rich soil with plenty of moisture during the growing season. They will form large clumps in the garden and are best left undisturbed.

C. asiaticum *Poison Bulb* This species comes from tropical Asia. It has a thick rosette of broad leaves to 120 cm tall with greenish-white fragrant flowers.

C. moorei Veldt Lily, Moore's Crinum A native of South Africa, this attractive large plant produces flower stalks almost 1 m high carrying heads of attractive pink lily flowers which are lightly fragrant. It prefers some shade.

C. pedunculatum Swamp Lily, River Lily This Australian native grows to around 1 m high and produces clusters of white scented flowers on stalks up to 80 cm long in early summer. Grow in a position sheltered from harsh sunlight.

Crocus

These early spring and autumn flowering bulbs with grass-like leaves and flowers of white, yellow and mauve are planted extensively in Europe and are most suited to areas with a cold winter. They derive their scientific name from the Greek *krokos*, meaning saffron. The commercial saffron long used for colour and flavouring comes from the dried orange stigmas of the saffron crocus, *Crocus sativus*. Crocuses require a cool position in a humus enriched soil with good drainage. Protect plants from hot sun and

Wallflowers

Violets

17

Freesias

Daffodils

winds. The bulbs like a dry resting period. Leave plants undisturbed until overcrowding compels lifting and dividing. The following species all have sweetly scented flowers.

C. biflorus **Scotch Crocus, Cloth of Silver Crocus** Grows to 10 cm with white to lilac flowers; some with purple veining. Flowers appear in spring.

C. chrysanthus A bright little plant to 7 cm tall with orange flowers feathered with bronze on the outside. Cultivars are numerous and include the buttercup yellow 'E.P. Bowles' and 'Snow Bunting' with white and cream flowers and dark lilac feathering. Flowers in winter.

C. imperati Grows to 8 cm tall with satiny purple flowers with a light fawn shade on the outside. Flowers in winter.

C. longiflorus The deep-lilac flowers with an orange throat are sometimes feathered on the outside. The flowers, which appear in autumn, are heavily scented.

C. sativus **Saffron Crocus** Grows to 12 cm high. The lilac flowers with darker veining and the famous stigmas are produced in autumn.

C. speciosus Bright lilac to purplish-blue flowers with darker veining grow on stems to 12 cm high. Flowers in early autumn.

Freesia refracta **Freesia** This is the old fashioned, highly fragrant, white-flowered species from which many colourful hybrids have been raised. They come in a wide range of brilliant colours although the scent of some of the hybrids has been diminished. The showy trumpet flowers are carried on wiry arching stems and are excellent for cutting. Plant bulbs in autumn in a fairly light but humus enriched soil. They like moisture, but good drainage and a sunny aspect. Freesias can be left in the garden for years and they will multiply happily. They are excellent for naturalising in grass and can be grown in containers.

Galanthus nivalis **Snowdrop** These are charming small bulbs with lightly fragrant bell flowers in late winter. They are often confused with the taller growing snowflake, but snowdrops are easy to identify since the three outer petals are pure white and much longer than the green-tipped inner ones. Plant bulbs in groups in early autumn in a porous good soil, preferably in a partially shaded position underneath shrubs and trees. They can be left undisturbed for years on end. The fragrance is very soft and it takes a good sized clump to scent the air. A cool climate is best.

***Galtonia candicans* Cape Hyacinth, Summer Hyacinth** This South African species is closely related to the hyacinth and was formerly named *Hyacinth candicans*. The white pendant bell shaped fragrant flowers are carried on tall spikes to 1 m high and bloom in late summer. Plant in a sunny position in good soil with good drainage. Grow in clumps for maximum effect and summer fragrance.

***Hedychium coronarium* White Ginger Blossom, Garland Flower** This beautiful clump forming plant to 2 m high comes from tropical Asia and is best planted in areas with a warm climate. The very fragrant orchid-like white flowers are borne at the ends of leafy stems during summer. Grow in a rich soil and provide plenty of water during the summer months. A semi-shaded position is preferred.

***Hedychium gardnerianum* Ginger Lily, Indian Garland Flower** This tall lush tropical-looking plant clothed with wide leaves bears large spikes of creamy-yellow flowers with prominent red stamens during the summer months. Flowers have a sweet spicy fragrance, and make spectacular large floral arrangements. Provide a well enriched soil in semi-shade with plenty of water during the summer months.

***Hyacinthus* Hyacinth** Hyacinths are among the loveliest of spring flowering bulbs with their beautiful sculptured blooms and powerful fragrance. The modern or Dutch hyacinths are improved forms of the wild species, *Hyacinthus orientalis*, and come in every shade of blue and mauve, pink, red, white and yellow, many of them double flowered. When buying hyacinth bulbs, ensure that they are solid, firm, heavy and large. Plant in autumn in a well drained, thoroughly enriched soil in a sunny position. The quality of the bulbs and flowers gradually deteriorates and replacements are needed every two or three years. Hyacinths are ideal for growing in pots and window boxes and containers for indoors. Pot bulbs in autumn in fibre or commercial potting mixture, the nose just above the surface.

Iris The name of this genus comes from the Greek *iris*, the rainbow goddess, and it is truly well named as the iris comes to us in all the colours of the rainbow and in all the combinations of colours and patterns. Iris fall broadly into three types: the bulbous type such as the Dutch, Spanish and English iris; the rhizomatous, bearded iris popularly known as flags; and the beardless iris which vary greatly in colour and form. Hybridists have been at work on the 200 natural species of iris and have raised cultivated varieties numbering many thousands. Not all are fragrant and the best way to discover those with a smell that appeals is to sniff those in bloom in exhibition, botanic and friends' gardens and make notes for future purchases. The bulbous *I. reticulata* and its many cultivars in shades of blue has fragrant flowers in late winter and early spring.

Orris root, the ancient fixative still used in potpourri preparation today, is the dried rhizome of the species, *I. pallida, I. florentina* and *I. germanica*. They are cultivated commercially in Italy on a vast commercial scale for use in the perfume industry. Although practically odourless when fresh, the dried rhizomes develop a sweet violet-like scent with time. Orris root may be bought in powdered form and provides an excellent fixative for potpourri, sachets and pomanders.

Leucojum vernum **Snowflake** These are the snowflakes of the early spring garden and are not to be confused with *Galanthus nivalis*, the true snowdrop. They grow to around 30 cm high and have delicate white bell flowers dotted on the outside with green. They are easy to grow and do well in any well drained soil, preferably in full sun or light shade. The dainty white flowers are beautifully perfumed and are delightful for small posies.

Lilium Lily
Lilies have been cultivated for their beauty since ancient times and have always been favourite garden plants. Today the original genus of around 80 species has been expanded to include hundreds of

new hybrids. Many of the lilies, especially those with white flowers, are beautifully fragrant and many make excellent cut flowers. Grow in a very well drained but not dry, humus enriched soil. Except for the Madonna lily, which must be planted with the top near the surface of the soil, cover the bulbs with at least 10 cm of soil. Most like shade around the roots, and in early spring and again in summer the clumps may be mulched with some rich organic compost or leaf mould as this will help flower production as well as keep the ground cool. Lilies are planted in autumn and winter. At no time must lily bulbs be allowed to dry out. When purchasing check that they are firm and have not been out of the ground for any length of time. Lilies can remain undisturbed for many years until it becomes quite obvious that they are overcrowded. When dividing clumps, remember that lily bulbs should not be stored or left out of the soil any longer than necessary.

L. brownii **Chinese lily** Grows to 1 m high with fragrant creamy-white trumpet flowers, shaded with purple and green, in early summer. Must have excellent drainage.

L. candidum **Madonna Lily** History tell us that, together with the damask rose, the Madonna lily was more often painted by medieval artists than any other flower, particularly in paintings of the Annunciation. In the early days of Christianity it was dedicated by the Church to the Madonna. It grows to around 1 m tall and produces a rosette of broad leaves and bears pure white trumpet flowers with curled back tips. Flowers are honey scented and appear in late spring.

L. longiflorum **November Lily, Christmas Lily, St Joseph's Lily** Native to Japan, this gardeners' and florists' favourite grows to around 1 m high. It carries delightfully fragrant funnel shaped flowers in November and early summer. It makes an excellent large container plant.

L. regale **Regal Lily** A popular and hardy species which grows to 1.5 m tall and bears narrow fragrant white trumpets with purplish streaks in summer.

L. speciosum Highly fragrant flowers are carried on sturdy stems to 1 m or more high. Flowers are white flushed with crimson and appear in late summer to autumn.

Muscari botryoides **Grape Hyacinth** Grape hyacinths are easy to grow spring flowering bulbs which will form attractive carpets if allowed to naturalise. They produce thin grass-like foliage and spikes of sweetly scented flowers arranged in conical heads in delightful shades of blue. Plant in autumn in a well drained, good soil in a sunny or partially shaded position. They look wonderful as edging plants, beneath shrubs and trees or in a container. Flowers in early spring.

Narcissus

This is the ancient Greek name of a youth obsessed by his own beautiful reflection and turned by the gods into a flower. *Narcissus* is the generic name of a large group which includes daffodils as well as jonquils. They have been cultivated since classical times and from the original 25 or so species up to 500 named varieties have been produced. Many of these offer a great variety of scents and a cheery clump of daffodils or jonquils never fails to bring joy to the onlooker.

Space does not permit a general description of all those with scented flowers and often what is pleasant to one person may be considered overpowering or unattractive by another. For example the popular golden trumpeted 'King Alfred' daffodil does not have the sweet fragrance of the jonquils, but for me its freshly mowed grass scent is the embodiment of spring and makes me want to immediately dig in the garden.

Of the daffodils with a noticeable sweet scent look for Poeticus and the Tazettas. Old Pheasant's Eye is pleasantly fragrant and is the last of all the daffodils to flower, coming into bloom during late October. Jonquils, with several flowers per stem, are noted for their highly perfumed flowers.

Daffodils are useful for planting between shrubs and under small trees, and look wonderful at random in grass. They are also ideal subjects for pot culture. Bulbs can be planted in threes and fives in commercial potting mixtures, providing that a sharp drainage medium such as charcoal is placed in a layer in the bottom of the container.

Bulbs should be planted in a slightly heavy, rich soil with excellent drainage. They will grow in partial shade or full sun. There is no need to lift the bulbs until they become overcrowded. Do not cut the leaves until they have died down, otherwise the bulbs will be weakened and future flowering impaired.

Polyanthes tuberosa **Tuberose** This old time garden favourite is widely grown commercially as a cut flower and source of perfume. Plant in a warm location in a rich well drained soil in full sun. Water well during the growing period. It will grow to around 1 m high and the long slender stems may need staking. The white wax-like blooms appear in summer. The beautiful fragrance is more penetrating in the evening air.

Sweet-scented Herbs

The herb garden is the oldest form of garden and the importance of herbs dates back thousands of years. Herbs have changed remarkably little over the years and many of the herbs we use today are the same ones used in ancient times. Most of us are familiar with some of the kitchen herbs, but lovers of fragrances will find in herbs a wealth of pleasing aromas that can be used in making potpourri or small posies. Most of the early medicinal herbs are no longer used in home remedies but are often included in the herb garden for their aromatic leaves, interesting textures and often attractive grey foliage.

Herbs are easy to grow and only require a small amount of care and attention. On the whole the sunniest site is best, with protection from strong winds and heavy frosts. Most thrive in a well drained light soil. If conditions suit grow herbs close to the kitchen. Apart from convenience, you can have the pleasure of seeing them from the house. Herbs delight the eye as well as the nose and mouth. Using herbs frequently in the kitchen greatly increases the pleasure of both cooking and eating. Many herbs can also be grown in containers. Ensure that drainage is perfect and that they do not dry out in hot or windy weather, especially if the container is small or porous.

Unlike most common plant names, those given to herbs are remarkably consistent throughout the English-speaking world. Herbs listed in this chapter are therefore listed under their English names first and their scientific names follow.

Basil, Sweet Basil *Ocimum basilicum* There are now a number of different varieties of basil available, enough to have quite an interesting collection. However, it is the annual basil with its wonderful fragrant leaves that is the most popular in cooking. Sow seeds direct in a sunny position when danger of frost is over. Pinch out stem tips frequently to encourage bushy growth and retard flowering and seeding. At the end of the plant's life seeds can be collected, allowed to dry and stored for next spring's planting. 'Dark Opal' has decorative purplish-bronze foliage and makes a beautiful basil vinegar.

Bay, Sweet Bay *Laurus nobilis* A very slow growing large shrub or small tree that may be planted directly in the ground or in a large container in a sunny sheltered position. Do provide good soil and drainage when growing in a container. The shiny green leaves possess a wonderful balsamic aroma that is more noticeable when dry. A bay leaf is one of the three herbs, with parsley and thyme, that makes up the classic bouquet garni. Once the plant is established, the leaves can be harvested at any time of the year and used fresh or dried for later use.

Bergamot, Oswego Tea *Monarda didyma* This very easy to grow perennial plant to around 1 m tall has strongly aromatic leaves and delightful scarlet flowers during summer. Flowers are rich in nectar and are beloved by bees which gives rise to another common name, bee balm. The leaves are used in potpourri and tea and as a flavouring.

Burnet, Salad Burnet *Pimpinella saxifraga* Burnet was one of the favourite herbs of the Tudors who used to plant it along pathways with thyme and chamomile so that its fragrance would perfume the air when walked upon. It is an attractive low growing perennial which requires plenty of sun. The pretty toothed leaves have a fresh, pleasant, cucumber-like flavour and are mainly used in a mixed green salad. Only fresh young leaves are used.

Catnip, Catmint *Nepeta cataria* Catnip is a perennial herb which may grow to 1 m tall. The downy oval leaves have a bitter fragrance and will scent the garden on a hot day or after a shower of rain. Plants will need cutting back each year after flowering to keep a good shape. Cats of course love this plant and soft prunings can be given to them as a treat to loll about and play in.

Chamomile *Anthemis nobilis* A low growing spreading perennial with daisy-like yellow and white flowers during summer. When

Monsieur Tillier tea rose, pineapple mint and oregano in containers

27

Basil

Thyme

Chamomile

Pelargonium graveolens

bruised or walked upon it emits a delightful fragrance and it has been used as a traditional ground cover over garden paths and walks and as a fragrant lawn. The dried blossoms make the soothing and delicious chamomile tea.

Chervil *Anthriscus cerefolium* Chervil is an annual with feathery leaves which have a pleasant light aniseed fragrance. Grow in a moist semi-shaded position. Cut away flowering stems to encourage fresh leaf growth and a longer supply. The leaves are used extensively in French cooking and is one of the herbs, with parsley, chives and tarragon, in the mixture known as *fine herbes* used to flavour omelettes. The young leaves are also used in salads.

Coriander *Coriandrum sativum* This small annual has pretty parsley-like leaves with a distinctive strong smell and taste that I think is delicious, but I know not all will agree. Young leaves freshly picked are an important ingredient in Asian, Mediterranean, Latin American and North African cooking. The dried small rounded seed with its spicy flavour is ground and used in curries. When buying seeds for cooking from an Asian shop, buy a large packet, save some for the kitchen and throw the rest in the garden. It has always worked for me and you get so much more than when buying seed packets. Sow seeds in spring in a sunny position in a light soil with good drainage. By sowing new seeds every two weeks you can have a continuous crop. Seeds are harvested in autumn when the seed heads are ripe. Allow to thoroughly dry out, then store in airtight containers.

Dill *Anethum graveolens* Dill is an annual with feathery light green leaves similar to fennel but shorter and smaller. Both leaves and seeds are pleasantly aromatic. Dill is grown direct from seed sown in spring in a sunny position. Fresh leaves are used in preparing fish and in salad dressings. The seeds are used to flavour pickled gherkins or a herb vinegar.

Fennel *Foeniculum vulgare* This tall perennial to around 2 m has delightful aniseed scented leaves, that are irresistible for pinching and sniffing when walking in the garden. Both the leaves and seeds have a pleasant flavour and are a good seasoning for fish, sauces and mayonnaise.

Lavender See Shrubs.

Lemon Balm *Melissa officinalis* A fragrant lemon scented perennial which forms an attractive spreading clump in a sunny or partially shaded position. The small white flowers are liked by bees which leads to the name *Melissa*, from the Greek for honeybee. The leaves of lemon balm are best used fresh in salads and to make a calming tea.

Lemon Grass *Cymbopogon citratus* This ornamental grass will add texture and interest to the garden as well as providing a sweet lemon fragrance. The dried leaves make a reviving cup of tea, but it is the white fleshy base of the leaves that is an indispensable ingredient in Thai and other Oriental cooking. It is best when used fresh.

Lemon Verbena *Lippia citriodora* A deciduous shrub to 3 m or more high with powerful lemon scented leaves that yield the verbena oil of commerce. Plant lemon verbena where it will have full sun with good drainage. The leaves retain their delicious lemony fragrance when dried and are an excellent potpourri ingredient. They also can be brewed into a tea.

Marjoram *Origanum majorana* This delightful perennial plant will grow in any well drained garden soil in full sun. Trim back if the plant spreads or prune to encourage fresh leaf growth. It also makes an attractive container plant. Marjoram, or its wild sister oregano, is an excellent herb for using fresh or dried. It goes well with many meats and can be sprinkled on salads.

Mint *Mentha* **species** There are many species of mint that you can grow to provide fragrance in the garden as well as fresh or dried mint for the kitchen. Spearmint, applemint and Bowles variety are all excellent for use in cooking, while eau-de-cologne mint and peppermint are excellent dried and used in potpourri. Both spearmint and peppermint can be used to make mint tea, a popular digestive taken after a meal. All the mints are perennials and most prefer a moist soil in a semi-shaded position.

Parsley *Petroselinum crispum* Apart from being indispensible in the kitchen, parsley is a most attractive plant for the garden with its decorative foliage and neat habit. It is a biennial that is grown from seed and does well in full sun or part shade in a moderately rich soil that is well watered during the growing period. Parsley is rich in vitamins and as with most herbs it is important to chop parsley at the last moment so that the full flavour is captured in the dish.

Pennyroyal *Mentha pulegium* This delightful fragrant ground cover can be grown along paths, in rocky crevices or spilling out of pots. It is a spreading perennial with runners that take root at the nodes and does well in moist, well composted friable soil. Very pretty lilac blooms appear in summer. Pennyroyal is said to repel insects from the garden and dried leaves are a good addition to moth repellent sachets for drawers and cupboards.

Rosemary *Rosmarinus officinalis* Since ancient times rosemary has had many medicinal uses and is also used in perfumes. It is the herb of remembrance. There are two main varieties of this delightful shrub—a prostrate form that is useful as a container, rockery plant or low hedge and the upright bushy form which grows to around 1 m high. All forms bear grey-green needle-like leaves that have a wonderful aromatic resinous scent. Rosemary likes a sunny position and good drainage. Pick regularly to encourage compact growth. The leaves, either fresh or dried, are used as a seasoning for grilled or roast meat, especially lamb and veal.

Sage *Salvia officinalis* A small perennial with grey-green velvety leaves and blue flowers during summer. The leaves have a distinct flavour and are used with pork and veal and in seasoning. Fresh leaves are preferable to dried. Grow in a well drained soil in full sun and allow to establish before taking too many cuttings.

Tansy *Tanacetum vulgare* This robust perennial dies down in winter and returns the following spring. It has bright green ferny leaves that yield an aromatic, slight lemony fragrance when crushed. Small buttonlike yellow flowers appear in late summer. In medieval times tansy was used for medicinal purposes but today it is used mostly as an insect repellent. Dried leaves can be used in anti-moth sachets. The dainty flowers are perfect for posies.

Tarragon *Artemisia dracunculus* French tarragon is one of the most important herbs used in French cuisine and should not be confused with the Russian tarragon which looks similar, except for rougher, greener leaves, and bears seeds. True tarragon does not produce fertile seeds and must be propagated vegetatively. Tarragon is a perennial with slender dark green leaves which have a delicious almost aniseed-like flavour. It works like magic with chicken and is excellent with lightly cooked vegetables. It is used in a wide variety of sauces and makes one of the best herb flavoured vinegars for salads.

Thyme *Thymus species* There are many species and varieties of thyme which are grown as ground covers, edging and ornamental plants. Most have aromatic foliage but it is *T. vulgaris* that is commonly used as a seasoning. The bush should be trimmed regularly to ensure healthy growth. Thyme leaves are most aromatic when young.

Wormwood *Artemisia absinthium* Wormwood is a perennial with woody stems to around 1 m high. It has silvery-grey finely divided leaves that have a bitter taste and pungent aroma. The best known use of wormwood was in making absinthe and it is now used as an ingredient in vermouth and liqueurs. It is a particularly attractive herb to grow and needs regular pruning to maintain good shape. Dry the foliage for use in moth repellent sachets.

Yarrow *Achillea millefolium* An attractive hardy perennial with pretty finely divided leaves that have a bitter fragrance when crushed. Flowers in white or deep pink appear in summer and autumn on tall stems. They are very useful for picking for indoors or should be cut back after they have finished blooming to ensure healthy growth.

Scented Geraniums

Of the many different kinds of geraniums (*Pelargonium* species), those best suited for the fragrant garden are the scented-leaved geraniums. Although most of these have small scentless flowers, they offer the widest range of perfumed foliage imaginable from peppermint to rose, nutmeg to apple and even coconut. Some offer their fragrance on a warm night or after a shower of rain, others need brushing past or a 'pinch and sniff' to release their wonderful scent. They also have interestingly textured and shaped leaves.

These are the geraniums of the old fashioned gardens our grandmothers knew. They grow readily from cuttings so it is easy to start a collection if you wish. Most nurseries stock them in the herb section. They like a well drained soil either in pots or in the garden and grow best in a sunny position. Pinch growing tips in the early stages to encourage side branching and a good shape, especially when growing in pots.

The leaves are ideal for picking and are lovely in indoor arrangements and posies. The peppermint geranium is especially attractive as its rather large velvety leaves make a perfect collar around a small posy. The leaves of the rose-scented geranium are used to flavour cakes, sugars and ice-creams. This geranium is grown in the south of France for the perfume industry, with rose-geranium oil being extracted from the leaves by a simple steam distillation process. Depending on your fancy all scented-leaved geraniums can be dried and used in potpourri mixtures, sachets and fragrant pillows. The prettiest shapes can be floated in finger bowls, or used to decorate summer drinks.

As most nurseries seem to sell scented geraniums by their English names I have chosen to list them here in that order with their scientific name (if any) following.

Apple-scented Geranium *P. odoratissimum* A small, slightly trailing plant with soft roundish ruffled leaves with a strong odour of apples when bruised. Tiny white flowers in fluffy clusters are borne on trailing stems.

Coconut-scented Geranium *P. grossularioides* A low growing trailing plant with dark green rounded leaves with scalloped edges. Leaves have a strong coconut fragrance. It bears clusters of tiny, rosy red flowers. Trailing habit makes this a good edging or hanging basket plant.

Lemon-scented Geraniums

P. crispum **'Major'** This delightful plant may reach 1 m high and has small, crinkly leaves with a very pronounced lemon scent and small lavender flowers.

P. crispum **'Variegated Prince Rupert'** This is a variegated form of the above mentioned species. It has very pretty frilled green leaves outlined in yellow. It is also sold as French Lace.

P. crispum **'Minor'** This small plant grows to around 60 cm tall with crowded, tiny ruffled lemony leaves and lavender flowers. It also has the marvellous name of Finger Bowl Geranium, so put it to good use.

Pelargonium × **'Mabel Grey'** This is one of the strongest and most fragrant of all the lemon-scented geraniums. It grows to an upright 1.5 m high bush and has a rather large leaf with a rough texture. Prune in spring to keep in shape and dry the leaves for use in potpourri.

Lime-scented Geranium *P. nervosum* This species grows into an attractive bushy plant to around 75 cm high. The round, light green leaves with toothed margins have the most pleasing fragrance of lime. The lavender flowers are abundant and showy.

Nutmeg Geranium *P. fragrans* A compact bushy little plant to no more than 50 cm high that looks well in a pot, trimmed to one inch of its life, as a tiny topiary. The dainty grey-green rounded leaves have a spicy, nutmeg-like scent and it carries tiny white flowers in summer and autumn.

Oak-leaf Geranium *P. quercifolium* This tall growing bushy species may reach 2 m. The large oak shaped leaves are rather rough and sticky to the touch. The perfume of the leaves is earthy and balsamic and is considered unpleasant by some. Its rightful place is in the garden as it has showy mauve flowers splotched with maroon. The leaves do not dry well and are not suitable for potpourri.

Peppermint *P. tomentosum* This is a lovely plant with attractive lobed velvety leaves that have a true peppermint fragrance. It has a rather trailing habit with tender stems and is best if allowed to tumble over a wall or out of a container rather than being forced into climbing, which it hates. Keep up the water in dry weather, especially if grown in a container.

Rose-scented Geranium *P. graveolens* This tall handsome plant to just over 1 m tall has slightly hairy, deep green lobed leaves, which are divided again and toothed. The leaves have a spicy rose-like fragrance and will retain their fragrance well when dried for potpourri. The small flowers are an attractive lilac-pink.

***P. graveolens* 'Lady Plymouth'** This is a smaller growing variety with finely cut leaves with pale cream edging and sometimes a splash of cream or pink. The scent is rosy with a hint of mint.

Australian Native Plants

Fragrance is one of the striking features of the Australian bush and it is the species with highly odoriferous foliage that give off the predominant aroma on a hot or rainy day. Our sense of smell plays a vital role in recalling to memory past experiences and most of us who have spent any time in the bush will quickly recall its distinctive spicy fragrance.

A wonderful way to capture the fresh sweet smell of the bush is to select and grow native plants with aromatic foliage. A large number of aromatic trees and shrubs have oil glands scattered over their leaves, sometimes extending to the young shoots, flowers and fruits. The glands are often translucent and appear like pin pricks if the leaves are held against the light. Many contain oil which is strongly aromatic and release their perfume when the leaves are bruised or on a hot day. Some such as the mint bushes emit their fragrance when watered or after a shower of rain, which gives us additional pleasure when watering the garden.

Australia is rich in plants with aromatic foliage, many of which belong to the myrtle family, Myrtaceae. Members of this large family include many hundreds of eucalypts, melaleucas, tea-trees, bottlebrushes, darwinias, kunzeas, thryptomenes, baeckeas, Geraldton wax and backhousias, which includes the lemon-scented backhousia, *Backhousia citriodora*. Other lemon-scented members are the widely cultivated lemon-scented tea-tree, *Leptospermum petersonii, Eucalyptus citriodora* and *Darwinia citriodora* which has a pungent lemon scent. Contrary to its botanic name, the crimson bottlebrush *Callistemon citrinus* does not have a pronounced lemon fragrance.

Other groups with aromatic foliage include the mint bushes, *Prostanthera* species, which belong to the same family as the kitchen mint, Lamiaceae. Some have pleasantly scented foliage, others have a pungent odour and some have no scent at all. When buying and selecting mint bushes it is best to give the foliage of the plant the 'crush and smell' test to see if you like the scent.

Prostanthera sieberi

Purple Mint Bush

Brown Boronia

Acacia spectabilis

Native Frangipani

Acacia floribunda

Angels' Trumpets *(Brugmansia suaveolens)*

This test can also be applied to members of the Rutaceae family which includes the boronias, croweas, eriostemons and zierias. Some species may have a pleasant fragrance of lemon, camphor or spice, others may smell of turpentine, old apples in the school bag or just awful. One species which springs to mind, *Zieria arborescens*, has the most appalling smelling foliage when freshly crushed. Strangely, when dried the leaves have quite a pleasant scent, although I haven't had the courage to include them in a potpourri. The common name of this plant is stinkwood.

Backhousia

A small genus of flowering shrubs and trees native to Australia. Most species have attractive aromatic foliage with transparent oil glands and showy clusters of small white flowers with conspicuous stamens. All species occur naturally in the rainforests of eastern Australia and grow best in mild climates with rich soil conditions and plenty of moisture.

B. anisata **Aniseed Tree** This attractive large tree grows to around 15 metres in cultivation. It develops a dense spreading crown of glossy green foliage that smells like aniseed when crushed. Abundant clusters of lightly perfumed flowers are produced in spring.

B. citriodora **Lemon-scented Myrtle, Lemon Ironwood** An ornamental shrub or small tree ranging from 3 to 8 m under cultivation. The dark green ovate leaves which are rather glossy in appearance have a strong lemon fragrance when crushed. Showy clusters of small white flowers literally cover the tree through the summer months. This species is slow growing and can be grown as a container plant. However it will not flower unless planted out in the garden.

B. myrtifolia **Grey Myrtle** A shrub or small tree to around 7 m in height. It has a dense bushy growth habit and neat glossy dark green leaves with a pleasant spicy odour when crushed. Clusters of small white flowers are produced during late spring and summer.

Baeckea

This genus contains around 70 species endemic to Australia. They are mostly small to tall shrubs with abundant tea-tree type flowers and decorative foliage. Quite a number of species have aromatic foliage when crushed, including the camphor-scented couple *B. camphorata* and *B. camphorosmae* and the lemon-scented baeckea, *B. citriodora*.

Boronia See Shrubs.

Chamaelaucium

This genus is confined in natural distribution to Western Australia and consists of around 20 species, all of which give off a pleasant aroma when the foliage is crushed. About four species have found their way into cultivation and are noted for their attractive and prolific flowering. The most famous of these is the Geraldton wax which has found worldwide recognition as a high quality cut flower and is grown commercially for this purpose.

C. uncinatum Geraldton Wax This delightful medium sized shrub can be bought in many different forms and flower colours range from white and shades of pink to reddish purple. Flowers are not fragrant, but do provide long lasting cut flowers for the house. The fine foliage has a refreshing scent and smells somewhat like 'Juicy Fruit' chewing gum when crushed. It is an irresistible pinch and smell plant in the garden. Other species of *Chamaelaucium* have similar scented foliage. Pruning for cut flowers or after flowering will keep the shrub in good shape.

Cymbopogon

There are about 8 Australian species in this worldwide genus of tussock forming grasses. The exotic lemon grass, *Cymbopogon citratus* of Sri Lanka and India, is grown on a commercial scale for production of lemon oil, which is distilled from the leaves. This is also the lemon grass found in many oriental recipes, especially in Thai dishes. The Australian species often have interesting and pleasant fragrances in the leaves and the attractive tussocks offer an appealing foliage contrast in the garden.

C. ambiguus Scent Grass, Lemon Grass An attractive blue-green grass which will form clumps up to 50 cm high. The leaves have a strong lemon-scented aroma. It makes an attractive rockery plant or accent plant for softening paved or walled areas such as driveways and courtyards. Grow in a well drained sunny position.

***C. obtectus* Silky Heads** A slender tall grass which will form erect tussocks up to 1 m high. The leaves have a spicy cardamom-like scent when crushed and were used by the Aborigines for medicinal purposes. Interesting silky flower heads are carried on stems up to 1 m tall during spring. Grow in a warm sunny location with good drainage.

Darwinia

Like a number of related genera in the family Myrtaceae, many darwinias provide an added charm in the spicy aroma stored in their leaves. The fragrance is readily released by simply brushing past the foliage of some species. There are about 60 endemic species, the majority found in Western Australia.

***D. citriodora* Lemon-scented Myrtle** This attractive rounded shrub has long been popular in cultivation. It grows to a height of 1 to 1.5 m and has a neat compact shape. The handsome foliage is arranged opposite in pairs along the stems and takes on most attractive bronzy tints in autumn and winter. The underside of the leaves is marked with numerous oil glands and when stems or leaves are crushed between the fingers a pleasant bitter lemon scent is released. Small orangy-red and green flowers are carried at branch ends in spring and summer. Provide excellent drainage in a lightly shaded position.

D. diosmoides This compact branched shrub may reach up to 3 m high. It has dark green, crowded heath-like leaves which are highly aromatic even when lightly brushed against. Small white to pink pin-cushion type flowers occur in spring and summer. Grow in full sun or part shade in a well drained position.

Eucalyptus

The genus *Eucalyptus* with its hundreds of species is undoubtedly the most important genus with aromatic foliage. Not all eucalypts emit the same familiar eucalyptus fragrance. Some leaves have a distinct fragrance of peppermint such as *E. piperita*, Sydney peppermint, and *E. nicholii*, the narrow-leaved peppermint. The composition of the oils varies from species to species as may be experienced simply by crushing the foliage and inhaling its perfume. A few species are important economically as a source of several different types of essential oils and various combinations are characteristic of particular species.

With the enormous range of eucalypts to choose from, space does not allow full description of all those with aromatic foliage. There are some excellent books available devoted to the cultivation of eucalypts and nursery people are usually more than happy to discuss species suitable to your area. When choosing a eucalypt for your garden it is best to think seriously about your site limitations before any other consideration. Remember that eucalypts are fast growing and many are too large for the average garden. The following is a quick reference guide to some species with highly odiferous foliage, including the expected size of the plant at maturity.

E. cinerea **Argyle Apple, Mealy Stringybark** Small to medium sized densely foliaged tree which may retain its branches to ground level. Ornamental juvenile rounded grey-green foliage is often retained at maturity. Excellent cut foliage for indoor decoration. 8 to 18 m high.

E. citriodora **Lemon-scented Gum** Medium to tall tree with magnificent white trunk and widely spreading open crown. Delightful lemon-scented foliage which is quite noticeable during hot weather. Early settlers used the foliage to scent linen and it is a good potpourri ingredient. 15 to 30 m high.

E. crenulata **Victorian Silver Gum** Small to medium fast growing tree with dense foliage. Attractive stem clasping juvenile foliage is grey-green. This is an excellent plant for providing long-lasting cut foliage for the house and for drying for potpourri recipes. Taking ample cut foliage or regular hard pruning will help retain the juvenile leaves and encourage dense bushy growth. 4 to 15 m high.

E. elata **River Peppermint, River White Gum** A small to tall tree with long narrow leaves and an open crown. It has a smooth white trunk except near the base. Its attractive pendulous habit makes it a beautiful specimen tree for medium to large gardens. 7 to 30 m high.

E. globulus **Tasmanian Blue Gum** Medium to tall tree too large for the average garden. Attractive oval grey-green juvenile foliage. The adult foliage is dark green, lanceolate and up to 30 cm long. Foliage is used in overseas countries for the distillation of essential oils. 15 to 55 m high.

E. nicholii **Narrow-leaved Black Peppermint** A small to medium tree with a slight pendulous habit and a dense spreading crown of attractive grey-green leaves that have a strong peppermint odour when crushed. This is a popular tree for parks and the home garden where space permits. 12 to 20 m high.

E. polybractea **Blue-leaved Mallee** A small multi-stemmed tree with attractive bluish leaves with prominent oil dots that have a distinctive eucalyptus aroma when crushed. The young growth of this species is regularly cropped and used commercially to produce a high quality essential oil. 4 to 10 m high.

E. radiata **Narrow-leaved Peppermint** Small to tall upright tree with highly aromatic leaves that emit a strong odour when brushed against. If space permits it is an excellent fragrant plant as its pervading scent will fill the garden on a hot day or after a shower of rain. Even the fallen dried leaves on the pathway, when crushed as you walk on them, will emit a lovely bush fragrance. 10 to 30 m high.

E. scoparia **Wallangarra White Gum** An attractive small tree with a slender pale grey trunk and an open crown of graceful weeping branches. The ornamental drooping narrow leaves are a shiny green and make this a beautiful specimen tree. 8 to 12 m high.

E. viridis **Green Mallee** This species may grow as a slender small tree or develop a characteristic mallee habit. It is a good tree for the smaller garden. It has highly aromatic narrow green leaves which are used for oil distillation in Victoria. 5 to 12 m high.

Leptospermum
These are the well-known tea-trees from which many of the colourful garden hybrids are now being cultivated. There are around 40 Australian species and some have aromatic foliage as one soon

discovers on a walk through the bush by giving the leaves the 'pinch and smell' test. In the early days of settlement the leaves of some species were used to make a substitute tea. The small open flowers are not fragrant, but are filled with nectar and are very attractive to bees and insect-eating birds. Tea-trees come in a variety of forms, sizes and shapes and it is best to confer with your nurseryman on the type most suited to your garden and area.

***L. petersonii* Lemon-scented Tea-tree** A large shrub or small tree to around 4 m high. Its small compact habit makes it a good tree for the small to average garden. The fine narrow foliage has a strong lemon scent when brushed against and on hot summer days will impart a lovely refreshing scent to the garden. The tree benefits from regular pruning which provides a good opportunity to collect the leaves for drying to use in a potpourri or added to the pot when making tea.

Mentha
Australia has about six species of mints which, like the kitchen garden mint, have the familiar minty scent. *M. diemenica* is the only species that seems to be available at some specialist nurseries.

Plectranthus
This large genus of around 250 species of perennials and shrubs is found in many tropical and subtropical regions of the world including Australia. Many have heavily scented leaves and are useful plants as they will grow in shade. They need a warm frost free climate. In cooler districts they can be used as indoor or glasshouse plants.

P. argentatus A robust spreading plant with large velvety grey leaves with a powerful sweetish scent. Pretty mint-like flowers are blue. This is an attractive ground cover for large areas.

P. graveolens A low growing, loosely branched shrub with heavily scented foliage and upright spikes of mauve flowers. Grow in a humus enriched soil.

Prostanthera
There are quite a number of mint bushes that are popular in

cultivation and although most do not have fragrant flowers many have aromatic foliage. On a warm day or after hosing or a shower of rain it is often the mint bushes that give the garden that wonderful fragrance of the Australian bush. They are best planted near the house or along a garden walk where the aroma can be enjoyed and the leaves pinched and sniffed at. Not all species have fragrant foliage and some have an unpleasant scent, so it is a good idea to 'smell before you buy'. Mint bushes require excellent drainage and thrive in a sheltered position. Prune after flowering to maintain compact bushy growth and ensure mass flowering the following spring.

P. cryptandroides This species was thought to be extinct until it was rediscovered in 1964 in New South Wales. It is a small dainty shrub to no more than 75 cm high with narrow sticky leaves which are highly aromatic. Masses of small mauve flowers are carried along the stems during spring, although some flowers can be seen at other times during the year.

P. incisa **Cut-leaf Mint Bush** A large showy shrub to around 2 m high with very aromatic oval toothed leaves. The lilac to purple flowers cover the bush during spring. It prefers dappled shade in a well drained position.

P. melissifolia **Balm Mint Bush** A tall bushy shrub to 3 m high. The dark green oval leaves are strongly aromatic. The violet or lilac flowers are carried in long open sprays at branch ends in early summer. There is a pink flowering form available.

P. ovalifolia **Purple Mint Bush** This is one of the hardiest and most popular species in cultivation with the most pleasant smelling leaves. It will reach about 3 m and benefits from a good pruning after flowering to encourage compact growth. Masses of purple flowers are produced in spring. There are also pink and white flowering forms and an attractive variety with purple-tinged foliage.

P. sieberi A slender shrub up to 2 m tall with dark green lobed leaves which have a powerful scent especially on a hot day or after a shower of rain. It requires plenty of water during dry weather.

The Fragrant Rose

It is hard to think of fragrance in the garden without thinking of the intense, intoxicating and delicious perfume of the rose. Roses are the world's favourite flower and since ancient times have been a symbol of beauty, love, fidelity and happiness. It is possibly the oldest plant known to modern man to be found in modern gardens. Fragrant old fashioned roses have been celebrated in song and legend throughout the ages and many have found their way into modern gardens and nurseries. Although some modern roses have been bred mainly for flamboyance and flower production, there are many which have a beautiful perfume.

There are so many different kinds of roses to choose from. They range in size from tiny miniatures to quick growing climbers, so you can always find a rose or two to suit a sunny position in your garden. It is a good idea to visit annual rose shows and specialist nurseries around late autumn and early winter when you can see the many beautiful roses available in bloom. This is the time you can see, smell, buy or order the rose of your choice. Many people who grow roses want varieties that are also good for picking for indoors. If you are looking for good cutting qualities, select ones with well shaped buds, long firm stems, a free flowering habit, perfume and long lasting blooms.

Roses are for anyone who loves gardening, whether on a large scale or in a small area. Careful placement in the garden will reward you with colour and fragrance for up to nine months of the year. It is no longer necessary to confine roses to a bare bed on their own, though generations of gardeners have told us that they are best grown this way. Interspersing roses with other plants is an effective way to use them if you do not have the space or do not care for a formal rose bed. Taller growing roses form the perfect backdrop for lower growing plants which will hide the bare legs of roses and provide contrast and something to look at and smell

Monsieur Tillier

Rosa 'Fragrant Cloud'

Rothmannia globosa

Gordonia axillaris

Magnolia grandiflora

Rosa 'Peace'

when the roses are not actually in flower. Low aromatic border plantings suitable for edging rose beds are thyme, lavender, sage and cotton lavender. Many of the spring flowering bulbs make good companions for roses. Iris look charming among roses; and lilies, which like the same growing conditions, will bloom all summer.

Gardeners with small or already crowded gardens may find that the best roses to grow are climbers which will reach up for their share of sunlight. Climbing roses are a diverse group, some have long running canes to 10 m, while some miniature climbers only grow about 1.5 m. Check this point with your nurseryman when buying. Ramblers with short stems are used for covering walls, banks, fences and pillars. Climbers, with stiffer canes than ramblers, do well growing on trellises or espaliered against a stark fence. They can be trained across a pergola and lend their own special magic to arbors.

The miniatures and other low growers are ideal as borders, in rock gardens or for beds filled with larger roses. They are wonderful for the small sunny courtyard or terrace garden where there is limited space. Miniature roses can also be grown in moveable pots, troughs, windowboxes, urns and baskets. When growing in containers it is important to repot them regularly into slightly larger pots in fresh soil as they get bigger. This is best done in winter when they are dormant. If left in small pots they will soon become root bound and dry out rapidly.

Hybrid Teas This is the largest and most popular type of rose. It was first developed in 1867 and has large flowers, mostly fragrant, carried usually one to a stem, but some may produce several. Hybrid teas are bushy and grow up to 1.5 m in height. They are very free flowering and bloom continuously from mid spring to late autumn. They have long stems ideal for cutting and cover an extremely wide colour range.

Floribundas These form a bush usually 1 m high carrying clusters of flowers in rich colours throughout spring, summer and autumn. Floribundas are similar in form to the hybrid teas, the only difference being that the floribundas carry more, slightly smaller flowers in multiple clusters. Interbreeding between the two types has blurred the distinction and many rose specialists now list them all together as bush roses.

Miniatures These are scaled down versions of hybrid teas and floribundas and range from 20 cm to 50 cm in height. They cover themselves with flower clusters from spring to autumn and are the ideal solution for rose lovers with limited space.

Standard Tree Roses These are simply bush roses grafted at the end of a tall strong single stem like a tree. They add elegant height to a garden and allow for underplanting.

Weeping Standard Roses These are climbers grafted in the same way as the standard rose, allowing their long flexible canes to weep gracefully from a crown around 2 m high.

Climbers Many modern climbers are bush rose varieties which have developed long rambling canes. They still retain their long flowering period and are always labelled Clg. (climbing) as in Clg. Peace and Clg. Iceberg. Rambling roses or pillar roses are a class with restrained habits for twining up and around vertical supports. They have short stemmed flowers held close to the foliage. Many of the beautiful old type climbers such as the Banksia roses flower only in the spring, but others carry on for as long as bush roses do. Always check flowering times when buying.

Old Fashioned Roses Many of the old roses do not have as long a flowering season as the modern bush roses, but in recent years have regained their popularity as many people restoring old houses want roses of the same period. The old roses make up for their short flowering period with their period charm, their fragrances redolent of old world gardens and, once established, their longevity. Quite a few do have repeat flowering. Some of these roses are superb garden plants with their soft, rich colours and interesting foliage. Another attractive feature is the decorative heps which can vary in size, colour and shape. Many of the specialist nurseries stock old roses and some have an amazingly wide variety to choose from. The best time to see them in flower at display gardens is during spring and early summer.

Shrubs for Fragrance, Foliage and Flowers

Shrubs can become a substantial part of garden design and help you change the shape of your garden. Their permanence lends character and distinction and many add the romance of heady perfumed flowers. They can be used decoratively in beds, borders, backgrounds or as specimens planted in the open ground or in a large tub. Shrubs can be planted between trees, as fill in plants of varying heights or used to form hedges or windbreaks. They will provide screening, privacy and shade. A shrub may be large or small and its mature height, shape and spread needs to be considered before planting. Each should be given plenty of space to develop and reach its full height and assume its natural habit of growth.

The choice of shrubs to perfume the garden is wide and, as with colour, fragrance in the garden needs to be handled with moderation. Put them all together and the effect could be quite overpowering with lovely individual scents squandered, especially in a small garden. Unlike some annuals and bulbs which need to be planted in masses to fill the air with scent, many of the shrubs are prolific bloomers and one good specimen may more than satisfy. Of course there are a variety of perfumed shrubs that flower at different times of the year and you could plant for year round fragrance. Spring perfume might include the mock orange, Mexican orange flower, heliotrope, lavender, lilac and virburnums. Some sweet scented summer flowering shrubs that fill the air with heady perfume are gardenia, night-scented jessamine, bouvardia and buddleia. For late winter scents who would be without the highly perfumed daphne or the very special fragrance of the brown boronia.

Acacia Wattle

Although we most often think of wattles as specimen trees which clothe themselves in fragrant golden blossoms in early spring, there are many smaller growing shrubby species which are equally fragrant. For taller varieties see the chapter on trees.

A. *boormanii* Snowy River Wattle This is a tall shrub to around 4 m with greyish stems which have a tendency to sucker. It has grey-green leaves and in late winter and spring has a spectacular showing of sweetly scented, bright yellow flowers which fill the air with fragrance for some distance. Provide good drainage and plenty of sun.

A. *buxifolia* Box-leaf Wattle An ornamental shrub to around 4 m high with small grey-green leaves and masses of scented golden-yellow ball flowers carried at the ends of branches in spring. This very adaptable species will thrive in most soils in a partially shaded or sunny position.

A. *cardiophylla* Wyalong Wattle This bushy shrub to around 4 m tall has a slight pendulous habit. It has ornamental finely divided leaves and bears wonderful sprays of sweetly scented golden ball flowers in spring. Grow in a well drained soil with plenty of sun. It benefits from pruning after flowering.

A. *myrtifolia* Myrtle Wattle A compact shrub to 2 m in height with attractive red stems and lovely pale lemon ball flowers with a very noticeable but pleasant fragrance. Flowers appear in late winter and carry through to summer. This species has a wide distribution and does well in most garden positions and climates.

A. *suaveolens* Sweet Wattle As its name suggests, this wattle has sweetly scented cream to pale yellow blossoms. Flowers appear throughout winter and early spring. It is a variable shrub, usually quite slender to around 2 m high. To encourage bushiness prune immediatley after flowering. It will grow in partial shade or full sun.

Boronia

There are about 95 species of boronia, mostly small to medium shrubs. Not all boronias have perfumed flowers, but most have aromatic foliage of the 'crush and smell' type. Some people consider the odour of some boronia leaves to be rather unpleasant, but when planted in the garden most of these will convey a refreshing bush fragrance on hot summer days or after a shower of rain.

Boronias do best in a very well drained soil that is rich in organic matter. It is important to keep the roots cool and protect against hot winds and excessive drying out. The application of a good mulch will help to provide a cool root run and keep an even soil temperature. To increase the life expectancy of the plant and to encourage bushiness boronias should be pruned well from their first year just after the flowering season. They make delightful long lasting cut flowers for the house. The flowers of the brown boronia can be dried and used in potpourri.

Bornia clavata This attractive Western Australian species is one of the easiest of the boronias to grow in the eastern states. It is a bushy shrub to around 1.5 m high with neat narrow foliage which is strongly aromatic. The dainty yellowish-green bell flowers have a light fragrance and bloom in late winter and spring.

B. denticulata This is a reasonably hardy species and one that is often offered for sale at nurseries. The bright pink flowers are not fragrant, but provide a wonderful display in late winter to spring. The light green narrow leaves are strongly aromatic and quite noticeable on a warm day or after a shower of rain. It grows to around 1 m high and can be grown in a container. Tip prune from early days to encourage compact growth.

B. floribunda **Pale-pink Boronia** A very pretty plant to around 1 m with reddish stems and aromatic pinnate foliage. The large shell pink flowers have a sweet perfume and are produced in spring. Grow in a partially shaded position and provide plenty of moisture, but good drainage.

B. megastigma **Brown Boronia** This is the all time favourite Western Australian brown boronia celebrated for its beautifully perfumed brown and yellow bell flowers. The flowers, which appear in late winter and spring, have for many years been grown commercially for cut flowers, and in Tasmania they are distilled for a very high quality essential oil. This is not the easiest boronia to grow and has a reputation for being short lived. It requires a continually moist, but well drained soil and needs cutting back after flowering to promote vigour and new growth. Grow in dappled shade and provide plenty of mulch to ensure that the root system is kept cool and moist. Some interesting colour variations are available at nurseries. All have beautifully perfumed flowers and all can be grown in containers for popping around the garden under windows, near doorways, on verandahs and in enclosed courtyards to capture that wonderful scent.

B. serrulata **Native Rose, Sydney Rock Rose** This delightful small plant is a favourite of many bush walkers around Sydney. It grows to around 1 m high with rich green aromatic leaves with finely toothed margins. The bright pink cup shaped flowers which appear in late winter and spring have a sweet soft scent not always detected on the plant. However a vase of these lovely flowers indoors will perfume a room. This species prefers filtered shade in the garden and a well drained soil, preferably in the shelter of larger plants.

Bouvardia longiflora **Scented Bouvardia** A small bushy shrub to around 1 m high which provides masses of white highly perfumed, star shaped flowers during summer. Grow in a rich warm well drained position and prune back hard after flowering to encourage compact growth. Do not grow in areas with frost. The colourful hybrids in shades of pink, salmon and red are not fragrant.

Brunsfelsia australis **Yesterday, Today and Tomorrow** A shapely bush to around 1 m high which at any one time during its flowering period may be covered with purple, mauve and white blooms of an extremely pleasant fragrance. Grow in light to filtered shade in a rich well drained soil. Does best in frost free districts.

Buddleia davidii **Butterfly Bush**
A vigorous upright shrub to 3 m high which will become dense if pruned regularly. In late summer it bears long trusses of fragrant lilac flowers which really do attract butterflies from afar. This is the parent of many named varieties. It needs good drainage and full sun.

B. globosa A rounded shrub to 2.5 m high with long pointed leaves with a felty undersurface. The attractive honey scented orange flowers in rounded heads richly perfume the air in early spring. Provide good drainage, full sun and plenty of water during dry weather.

***Cestrum nocturnum* Night Jessamine, Night Flowering Cestrum** This is a straggly wiry shrub that may reach 3 m high, but will improve in shape if kept well pruned from early days. The greenish-white flowers are borne in clusters and have a powerful strong fragrance at night during summer and early autumn. Its perfume is almost intoxicating and some people find it too overpowering if planted near windows or doors.

***Choisya ternata* Mexican Orange Flower** This compact plant to 2 m has attractive evergreen glossy leaves and beautiful white flowers with an orange blossom fragrance all through spring. Sometimes it flowers again in later summer or early autumn. Provide a rich well drained soil in a sheltered sunny position.

***Daphne odora* Sweet Daphne** This shrub is one of the joys of the winter fragrant garden. It will reach about 1 m in height and has small waxy flowers red or pink in bud, opening to white or faintly pink. Daphne requires excellent drainage in a soil enriched with organic matter such as manure, compost or leaf mould. It will not tolerate lime. Grow in partial shade preferably facing east, in a sheltered position away from hot winds and afternoon sun. A few sprigs picked for indoors will quickly pervade a room with its lovely sweet fragrance. Although this is the most widely grown species, there are other species and varieties with variegated foliage available that also have beautifully perfumed flowers.

Gardenia
These handsome shrubs with attractive glossy leaves and heavily fragrant white flowers are a favourite with florists, gardeners and brides. They are widely grown in the open ground where there is a warm to hot climate and in cool areas gardenias are a treasured greenhouse plant. They do best in a rich, slightly acid soil and need plenty of water and feeding to produce their wonderful opulent looking flowers.

G. jasminoides **'Florida'** This attractive branching shrub may reach 2 m in height with equal spread. It bears deliciously fragrant white double flowers that will sweeten the summer air and may bloom into autumn. They are excellent as cut flowers.

G. jasminoides **'Radicans'** This is a low growing gardenia with slightly smaller flowers and leaves which can be used to advantage in a rock garden, spilling over walls or in a container on a patio or courtyard. Provide a little shade to prevent burning of buds.

G. thunbergii A slow growing shrub or small tree which usually only reaches around 2 m high. It is more tolerant of cool conditions and bears lovely tubular flowers opening to white saucer shaped single flowers usually in autumn. These are richly scented.

Hamamelis mollis **Chinese Witch Hazel** This is a large hardy deciduous shrub which sheds its leaves in autumn before producing fragrant golden flowers set on bare crooked branches throughout the winter. When cut these flowers make beautiful winter arrangements. Grow in a humus enriched soil that does not dry out.

Heliotropium arborescens **Cherry Pie** A soft wooded sprawling shrub with finely wrinkled leaves and small heads of highly scented lilac or purple flowers in summer and autumn. Pinch back and regularly prune to keep in shape. Grow in a rockery or garden bed among annuals and perennials. It will do well in a container and can be used in hanging baskets.

Lavendula **Lavender**
Prized for their perfumed flowers and aromatic foliage, the lavenders are beautiful natives of southern Europe and the Mediterranean countries. Several species yield lavender oil used in perfumery, the kind distilled from *Lavendula angustifolia* being considered the finest. Lavender is easy to grow and will flourish in a well drained sunny position. Flowers are long lasting in arrangements and can be dried for use in potpourri or sachets.

L. angustifolia (**syn.** *L. officinalis*) This dwarf shrub which occurs naturally in the southern French Alps is grown commercially in Tasmania for its high quality lavender oil. This species has thin,

Daphne odora 'Rubra'

Gardenia jasminoides 'Florida'

Lavendula stocchas ssp. *pedunculata*

Murraya paniculata

63

Beaumontia grandiflora

Gelsemium sempervirens

Hoya carnosa

Wisteria sinensis 'Alba'

smooth edged leaves and long thin spikes of blue-purple flowers with a strong characteristic fragrance. It flowers only during summer.

L. dentata **French Lavender** This lavender is the one best known to us in gardens with its toothed grey-green leaves and spikes of mauve flowers which appear for most of the year. It is a strong grower to around 1 m tall and can be trimmed into a dwarf hedge or allowed to grow naturally.

L. stoechas **Italian Lavender** This species is also known as French, Spanish or bush lavender, and is a good example of the need for using scientific names. It is a low shrub to 60 cm high with narrow leaves and deep purple flower spikes, mostly in spring. It is a prolific flowerer, but flowers are not as highly perfumed as the others.

Michelia figo **Port Wine Magnolia** A glossy leaved evergreen shrub to 3 m which does well over a wide climate range. It bears creamy-pink flowers like small magnolia blossoms with an unusual strong fruity fragrance. These appear in spring to early summer and will fill the garden with their sweet scent. Grow in a partially shaded position in a moist rich soil.

Murraya paniculata **Orange Jessamine** A lovely obliging shrub to around 2 m high with dark green glossy foliage which makes for an attractive densely foliaged plant. However it is the masses of orange blossom type flowers, with their wonderful jasmine-like perfume, that make this a delightful shrub to grow for fragrance in any garden. It flowers in spring, summer and autumn. It likes a warm climate and does best in a semi-shaded position in a humus enriched soil with plenty of water.

Philadelphus coronarius **Mock Orange** A deciduous shrub, 2 to 3 m high, with long arching branches carrying masses of saucer shaped white flowers with an orange blossom fragrance in early summer. Does well in temperate areas in sun or partial shade. Pruning, if necessary, should be done after flowering.

Syringa vulgaris **Common Lilac** This is one of the loveliest of deciduous flowering shrubs, growing to around 2.5 m with a tree-like habit and true lilac flowers with a strong sweet fragrance. Most of the named varieties are hybrids of this species with a colour range from pure white through palest lavender to dark purple and red. Both single and double flowered varieties are available. Lilac needs a fairly cold winter to do well. Being deciduous it is best planted in winter in a moderately rich, well drained garden soil that has a fairly high lime content. Provide a good mulch in summer to keep the roots cool. Prune moderately immediately after flowering to remove dead flower heads.

Viburnum

These highly ornamental shrubs or small trees are grown for their showy, often heavily perfumed flowers, attractive foliage and brightly coloured berries which often persist into autumn and winter. They are easily grown in a rich well drained soil with plenty of water during summer. Prune only lightly immediately after flowering to shape.

V. × burkwoodii A strong growing semi-evergreen to 2 m high with an open habit. Leaves often colour well in autumn and may be sparse in winter. The flattish clusters of white flowers are pink in bud and sweetly fragrant, appearing in late winter and spring.

V. carlesii A deciduous shrub to 1.5 m or more with a rounded habit and downy leaves often colouring in autumn. The rounded clusters of waxy white strongly fragrant flowers are pink in bud and bloom in spring. This highly perfumed shrub does best in a cool climate.

V. suspensum An evergreen to 2.5 m high with oval shaped shiny leaves and fragrant creamy-white to pink flowers followed by red berries.

Climbers

Apart from providing variety of outline in a garden, climbers are ideal in small gardens where there is not much growing space on the ground. You can have fragrant delights by training a climbing plant along the edge of your verandah or up a trellis or allowing it to cascade out of window boxes bringing wonderful scents into the house. Climbers occupy vertical space and can be used to outline a special feature such as an arch, arbor or pergola. They will disguise an unattractive wall, soften harsh architectural lines, hide an unpleasant view or cover an old garden shed or garage. They are invaluable for covering a boring old grey paling fence or a newly constructed wire mesh fence.

Trellis work provides support for climbers as well as being an interesting feature in the garden. It will also enable you to secure privacy and shelter from the wind and harsh sun and can be obtained either in a horizontal or diagonal pattern. As climbers become heavier as they mature the support you choose must be such that it will last as long as possible and should be in place before planting.

Determine if the climber you want is to be evergreen or deciduous. Both have advantages. A deciduous climber over a pergola or along a verandah will provide you with summer shade, but allow light and sun to penetrate during winter. Evergreen climbers are best suited to an area which needs quick cover or a permanent screen for privacy. All climbing plants benefit by the removal of the older wood and wayward stems to make room for more vigorous young growth.

Beaumontia grandiflora **Herald's Trumpet, Nepal Trumpet Flower** A magnificent robust climber from the Himalayas which needs good support for its vigorous growth. It is an evergreen with large leaves and large, trumpet shaped white flowers that are beautifully fragrant. It is suitable to warm climates only as it is tender to frost. Grow in a rich deep soil and prune immediately after flowering.

***Gelsemium sempervirens* Carolina Jasmine, Yellow Jasmine** An evergreen climber with small glossy leaves and fragrant yellow flowers which appear for many months in autumn, winter and spring. This is a pretty climber that is neat in its early years, but needs to be kept in check in limited spaces. It needs some support initially and does well in most mild climates.

***Hoya carnosa* Wax Flower** This evergreen climber with thick fleshy leaves bears rounded heads of pale pink waxy flowers which are sweetly fragrant. Easy to control, it is suitable for growing outdoors in warm, frost free areas and flowers best in a container where it can become pot bound. Dead flower heads should not be pruned as new flowers form on the remains of the old ones.

Jasminum Jasmine
It is perhaps for their fragrance more than anything else that jasmines are planted and some species are important in the making of perfume and jasmine tea. Many are evergreen climbers or trailers and are hardy in most situations in either light shade or full sun. Grow to adorn walls, to frame doorways or in any position near the house so the perfume can be enjoyed.

J. azoricum This fast growing, but well behaved climber from Madeira, to around 2 m, can also be trained as a shrub. It has white, wax-like perfumed flowers in summer and autumn.

***J. grandiflorum* Poet's Jasmine** A manageable climber to around 3 m with large leaves and beautiful, white scented flowers which occur singly for a good part of the year.

J. polyanthum This vigorous climber is the jasmine well known to us all for its beautiful trusses of white heavily scented flowers, which are deep pink in bud. It is the most fragrant of the jasmines, but receives criticism for its untidiness when the flowers fade and its ability to root easily and take over the garden. If space is limited it is best to confine this jasmine to a large container.

Lonicera Honeysuckle

This is a large genus of shrubs and creepers known for their showy flowers, which in many cases are sweetly fragrant. Support climbing forms, which look beautiful scrambling over fences and walls. They are tough and quick growing and all do well in moist conditions.

L.* × *americana This evergreen climber can be supported as a climber or trained into an attractive shrub or hedge. It has slender yellow tubular flowers with attractive red buds. The fragrant flowers, borne in terminal whorls, are produced in spring and are lovely for picking.

***L. japonica* Japanese Honeysuckle** A vigorous evergreen climber with creamy white flowers ageing yellow. Flowers are fragrant and are borne in pairs in spring. This is a rampant climber and is best suited to large areas or confined to a container to keep under control.

L. japonica* var. *aurea-reticulata This variety is the same as above, but has outstanding foliage of oval green leaves with a network of gold veins.

***L. periclymenum* Woodbine, English Honeysuckle** A deciduous climber which becomes bushy. It bears highly fragrant, creamy-yellow flowers on bare branches before the new leaves. Flower buds are tinged with purple.

***Mandevilla laxa* (syn. *M. suaveolens*) Chilean Jasmine** This vigorous twining vine may be deciduous in cold areas. It is fast growing in warm climates when given rich soil and plenty of water. The white, funnel-shaped flowers are highly fragrant and good for picking. Flowers in summer for a long period.

Rosa Rose

These are discussed in a separate chapter. They should not, however, be overlooked when selecting fragrant climbers, creepers and ramblers. Roses suit arbors, archways, fences, pergolas or, with a bit more work, can be espaliered along brick walls.

***Stephanotis floribunda* Madagascar Jasmine** This pretty evergreen climber has thick shiny leaves and wonderful sprays of white waxy flowers with a strong perfume. The flowers are long lasting when cut and are a favourite wedding flower. It is best planted against a wall or trellis for support and does well in a container.

***Trachelospermum jasminoides* Star Jasmine** A comparatively slow growing twining plant with neat lustrous foliage and flowers which very conveniently bloom in summer when the other jasmines have finished. Masses of fragrant, white star-like flowers are carried in dainty clusters. Provide support for the twining stems and lightly prune regularly to encourage neat growth. This species also makes an excellent ground cover and is attractive tumbling over stone walls.

Wisteria

Among the most popular deciduous climbers are the romantic wisterias. They are grown for their large drooping sprays of violet-blue flowers during spring. Although they take some time to establish, they soon become large vigorous plants and should be given very strong support. They are beautiful when planted covering a walkway or pergola with the pendulous flowers hanging overhead.

***W. floribunda* Japanese Wisteria** A vigorous vine with long stems to 10 m or more and very long flower clusters up to 1 m in length. Flowers are most commonly violet to purple-blue, however they also come in shades of white, purple and pink.

***W. sinensis* Chinese Wisteria** A large vigorous vine to 30 m with flower sprays opening just before or with the young soft leaves. Although the blue flower sprays are shorter than the previous species they are the most fragrant. The white flowering variety of this species is especially attractive and fragrant.

Tantalising Trees

Trees are the backbone of our garden as well as the backbone of life itself. They play a vital role in the ecological balance and are continually engaged in purifying the air we breathe and contributing to the world's rainfall. They help control erosion, provide cooling shade, act as sound barriers, give privacy, beauty, shelter for birds and offer nectar for animals and insects.

Without trees and other plants, life on this planet would cease to exist. By planting trees you are not only controlling your own pleasing environment, you are helping to create a better climate. Apart from the practical gains, trees offer fragrance and colour and many have attractive and aromatic foliage.

Every garden needs at least one tree. As trees remain in one particular position find out the ultimate size of the tree and its suitability for conditions in your garden. In small areas width may be of more importance than height. Deciduous trees are often useful here as they allow sunshine into the yard during winter.

Acacia Wattle
There are many taller growing wattles suitable for large or small gardens and for a wide range of climatic conditions. In general, wattles are very fast growing, but compared to many other trees are not long lived—say ten to fifteen years depending on the species and growing conditions. They will provide quick shade and many are beautifully perfumed. Pruning should be done immediately after flowering for shaping and to help prolong the life of the plant.

Acacia baileyana Cootamundra Wattle
This widely cultivated ornamental tree has delightful silvery-grey foliage and masses of bright yellow blossoms in dense clusters at branch ends during late winter and early spring. Flowers are sweetly scented and attract insectivorous birds to the garden. For use in the larger landscape as an attractive specimen tree. It is frost hardy.

71

A. decurrens **Early Black Wattle** This is a spectacular tree when in full bloom in late winter. It may reach 15 m in height with a shapely crown of golden blossoms with a noticeable sweet fragrance. It is very fast growing, but is subject to attack by borer which may shorten its life.

A. floribunda **White Sallow Wattle** A lovely small tree to around 7 m with a slight weeping habit. It has narrow foliage and pale lemon flowers arranged in loose spikes. Flowers appear in late winter and spring and their strong scent will fill the air for some distance. A very hardy and easy to grow wattle.

A. longifolia **Sydney Golden Wattle, Sallow Wattle** A fast growing small tree to 5 m with long golden spikes of flowers in late winter and early spring. The flowers are prolific and delicately scented. It is usually fast growing and will thrive in most well drained soils and situations.

A. prominens **Golden Rain Wattle, Gosford Wattle** A most attractive and long lived species with grey-green foliage. The long slender branches are massed with fragrant lemon flower balls in early spring. Grows to 20 m.

A. pycnantha **Golden Wattle** This beautiful pendulous small tree to 10 m bears a profusion of large, deep gold, scented flower balls during spring. This is Australia's floral emblem. It is popular in cultivation where it will grow in most well drained soils and conditions. It is frost tender while young, but fairly drought hardy.

A. spectabilis **Mudgee Wattle** A beautiful shrub or small tree to 5 m with feathery grey-green foliage. The bright yellow sweet-scented flower balls are carried on long sprays in late winter and early spring. This adaptable species will grow in most well drained soils in a sunny position and will withstand frost and periods of dryness. Lightly prune after flowering to shape.

Brugmansia

A genus of shrubs and small trees grown for their wonderful dangling trumpet shaped flowers which are highly perfumed, especially at night. They were previously known as *Datura*. The leaves, flowers and seeds of all species are poisonous. They are suitable for most areas except those with heavy frosts. Protect from winds and provide plenty of water in summer.

B. × *candida* (syn. *Datura cornigera*) A tall shrub or small tree from 3 to 6 m with velvety grey-green leaves and many large pendant, trumpet shaped flowers of white or shades of pink and cream. These appear mostly in summer and are beautifully fragrant at night.

B. *suaveolens* Angel's Trumpet This fast growing tall shrub or small tree to 6 m has long white flowers, sometimes shaded green, yellow or pink. They bloom in summer and autumn and their strong scent is most apparent in the evenings.

***Calodendron capense* Cape Chestnut** This prolific flowering tree may reach up to 20 m high. It bears dense clusters of pale pink flowers, conspicuously dotted with maroon spots, mostly during summer. Flowers are highly fragrant and suitable for picking. Plant in a rich, well drained soil and provide plenty of water.

Citrus When choosing fragrant trees for the garden don't overlook the wonderful variety of citrus plants that are available. Apart from providing you readily with fruit you would normally have to buy, all bear beautifully perfumed waxy white flowers. Citrus fruits are the easiest and most commonly grown fruit-bearing plants in the home garden and include oranges and lemons, grapefruit, limes and mandarins. All are attractive and their brightly coloured fruits lend a highly decorative element to the garden. All citrus trees can be planted in containers provided the pot is large enough.

***Dais cotinifolia* South African Daphne** This very attractive, semi-deciduous shrub or small tree may reach 4 m or more where conditions suit. The mauve-pink flowers are borne in rounded heads and will completely cover the tree in late spring. Their lovely fragrance is especially noticeable at dusk.

***Dombeya tiliacea* Natal Cherry** A small tree to 8 m which produces showy clusters of perfumed white flowers at the ends of the main and side branches during autumn. Grow in a light sandy soil enriched with compost or organic matter. Shelter from strong wind and frost.

Drimys winteri **Winter's Bark** A decorative evergreen tree to around 6 m tall. The leathery leaves and young red bark have a pleasant peppery aroma. The white fragrant flowers, borne in clusters, have the perfume of jasmine. Does best in moist, well drained conditions in a frost free climate.

Gordonia axillaris **Gordonia** This hardy shrub or small tree to 10 m high has attractive thick, shining leaves and white camellia-like flowers with golden stamens during autumn and winter. They have a light refreshing scent. This is a lovely shrub for areas free of frost.

Hymenosporum flavum **Native Frangipani** This beautiful Australian tree is well known for its delightfully perfumed cream flowers which will scent the air for some distance when in full bloom. It will reach up to 15 m in cultivation and has shiny bright green leaves. The cream flowers are tubular in shape and are carried in great profusion in late spring. It is fast growing and prefers a warm climate. Provide good drainage and a rich soil.

Magnolia
Magnolias are amongst the most popular of the late winter and spring flowering trees. They are fairly hardy and like a position with full sun and plenty of water in summer. Shelter from direct winds, especially the deciduous magnolias, as the delicate flowers will not survive otherwise. Provide good drainage and a good humus enriched soil. An annual mulch of leaves or other organic matter will prevent the soil from drying excessively in summer.

M. denudata **Yulan** This beautiful tree to 6 m or more in height produces the most superbly fragrant flowers. Before the leaves appear, its branches are studded profusely with creamy-white tulip shaped flowers at the end of winter. This is a parent of many excellent hybrids.

M. grandiflora **Evergreen Magnolia, Bull Bay** This is a large evergreen tree sometimes reaching 25 m high with a very generous spread. The glossy dark green leaves have a felty undersurface and very large open creamy-white fragrant flowers are produced in mid summer.

M. stellata **Star Magnolia** This shrub-like magnolia which grows to around 3 m high is ideal for the smaller garden. The flowers are white and fragrant, with many narrow petals and have a flattened daisy-like appearance. They are among the first magnolias to flower in late winter and are borne profusely even on young plants. There are several varieties available with flower colours ranging from shell pink to reddish purple.

Melia azedarach **White Cedar, Persian Lilac** A very attractive fast growing deciduous tree to around 12 m tall. In spring along with the new foliage it produces a beautiful crop of delightfully fragrant lilac flowers. On a warm night the perfume can be quite noticeable some distance from the tree. Flowers are followed by yellow berries which remain on the tree for some time. This adaptable hardy tree will grow in most soils and conditions including hot, dry districts. It will also withstand frost.

Osmanthus fragrans **Sweet Olive** A tall shrub or small tree with glossy oval leaves. For a long period during summer it bears tiny white flowers which give off a pervasive sweet fragrance of apricots, detectable some distance from the plant. Grow in a rich well drained soil in a partially shaded position. In Asia the flowers are used to perfume tea, which explains its other common name, tea olive.

Pittosporum

A number of pittosporums are grown as ornamental small trees for their attractive foliage, colourful berries and fragrant flowers. Most are hardy and trouble free but may have a tendency to white wax scale and leaf scale, so it is a good plan to spray regularly.

P. crassifolium **Karo** A compact small tree to 5 m with thick oval leaves and terminal clusters of fragrant brown flowers in spring. A smaller variegated variety with bright cream-margined leaves grows to around 3 m. This species will withstand drought and salt spray and is ideal for the seaside garden.

***P. eugenioides* Tarata** A native of New Zealand, this popular plant in cultivation forms a shapely, upright tree to 12 m or more. It has sweetly aromatic light green leaves with wavy edges and a lemon scent when crushed. The small yellowish fragrant flowers are carried in dense clusters. A handsome variegated form with cream-margined leaves also has small fragrant flowers.

***P. undulatum* Native Daphne, Sweet Pittosporum** This fast growing Australian tree is widely cultivated in the eastern States where it grows to around 10 m or more. It has large glossy wavy leaves and clusters of creamy white flowers in spring with a strong daphne-like fragrance. Flowers are followed by orange berry-like fruit.

***Plumeria acutifolia* Frangipani** This is the species most often seen growing in warm Australian gardens. It is a fast growing deciduous tree to around 8 m or more in hot climates. Most of the large leathery leaves are carried in whorls near the tips of the stout fleshy stems. The showy white or pink flowers with a yellow throat have a beautiful sweet perfume and remain fresh for a long time, making them the favoured lei flower of Hawaii. In temperate gardens flowering begins in summer and is carried through to around Easter. *P. rubra* has deep pink flowers with yellow centres and shorter, rounded leaves. Grow in a well drained soil in frost free districts.

***Rothmannia globosa* Tree Gardenia** More of a tall shrub, to 3 m high, than a tree. The waxy leaves may be part deciduous at flowering time. The long bell shaped flowers are creamy-white in colour and have a beautiful gardenia-like fragrance. These appear in spring and the perfume is very pervasive, especially in the evenings. The flowers are followed by persistent round pods which can give the tree an untidy appearance. For warm districts. Grow in a rich soil in a sheltered sunny position and provide plenty of water.

Potpourri

One of the joys of making your own potpourri is the added excuse to escape to and dally in your garden collecting and drying the plant material available to you. With our hectic way of life making potpourri is a most satisfying and therapeutic pastime which adds an extra dimension to the enjoyment of gardening. A potpourri will freshen and perfume your home in a most natural way and makes a very acceptable gift. Also a well made, home grown mixture is usually far superior to most potpourris available commercially. They are often made of imported dried flowers with a dose of floral essence which quickly fades. Or worse, they are scented with essence of strawberry or peach and tarted up with dyed flowers or wood.

Your fragrant garden can easily provide almost all the ingredients necessary to make a lovely fragrant mixture. You will need to raid the kitchen cupboard for a few spices to help the potpourri hold its scent and to contribute to the overall fragrance of the blend. A fixative such as oakmoss or orris root will help to preserve and stabilise the perfume. If you want to strengthen the scent of your potpourri you may wish to purchase a few essential oils. Fixatives and essential oils can be obtained from some chemists and health food shops.

A good potpourri should always smell wonderful and should keep its fragrance for a long time. This is easy to achieve if you ensure you are using the best quality plant material and everything is absolutely bone dry before you start. Any dried ingredients that show any sign of mildew should be discarded. For the potpourri maker a very long spell of wet and humid weather spells disaster.

Drying

Pick flowers and foliage on a dry day, preferably after a dry spell. Try to remember not to water the garden the day before and never use any plants that have been sprayed with pesticide. Roses need to be plucked and the petals spread for drying. Other fragrant flowers such as lavender, sprigs of wattle, dianthus, violets, honeysuckle, wallflowers and citrus blossoms can be plucked from their stems and dried whole. These are best spread in a single layer on either sheets of newspaper, shallow cardboard boxes, flat baskets or special drying racks, if you want to get really involved. If possible place in an elevated position for good air circulation and leave in a darkish, airy, warm room until dry. Stir or toss the petals when you think of it to encourage even and faster drying.

Foliage and herbs can be dried quickly and easily by tying the branches loosely together and hanging in a shady but airy room. A dark hallway where the bunches can capture the breeze from an open door is excellent. When crispy dry, strip off all the foliage before storing. All plant material should be stored as soon as it is dry, otherwise it will fade in colour and lose more of its fragrance to the air. If it rains it will sponge up the moisture from the atmosphere and seem to take forever to dry. Store each species separately in a labelled airtight container until you have enough ingredients to make a batch of potpourri.

Sweet Spring Potpourri

This recipe does not need to be followed exactly and may be adapted to what is available from your garden. All measurements are of dried flowers and foliage.

3   cups rose petals
1   cup lavender flowers
3   cups of any or all of the following: freesias, honeysuckle, cottage
     pinks, violets, citrus blossom, wallflowers
1   cup each lemon verbena leaves and rose geranium leaves
½   cup whole allspice, lightly crushed
1   tablespoon each of coarsely ground cloves and crumbled
     cinnamon sticks
½   cup orris root powder
8   drops rose oil
6   drops rose-geranium oil

1   cup of blue flowers for colour and decoration which might include whole cornflowers, delphiniums, larkspurs, borage flowers and a few pressed pansies

Combine all dry ingredients except the pressed pansies. Add the oil a drop at a time, mixing through thoroughly with your hands as you add. Place in an airtight container and allow to cure for six weeks. Transfer to ceramic or glass containers and decorate with the pressed pansies. This potpourri is also lovely in an open bowl with the pressed pansies on top.

Aromatic Potpourri

A refreshing potpourri made without flowers.

2   cups eucalyptus leaves of your choice
1   cup lemon verbena foliage
1   cup rosemary leaves
1   cup lemon-scented tea-tree leaves
½   cup thyme
½   cup each dried lemon and orange peel, chopped and lightly crushed in a mortar
½   cup coriander seeds, lightly crushed
1   cup fragrant wood shavings
1   cup oakmoss
5   drops rosemary oil
5   drops bergamot oil
      gumnuts, sprigs of wattle or small paper daisies for decoration

Place all the dried foliage in a large mixing bowl and lightly scrunch with your hands as you mix. In a separate bowl combine the citrus peel, coriander seeds, wood shavings and oakmoss. Add the essential oils to this mix and rub through with your fingertips making sure the oil is thoroughly blended. Store in an airtight container for about a month to mature. Transfer to glass jars or open bowls and decorate with gumnuts, sprigs of wattle and paper daisies.

Index